SHELLING PEAS WITH MY GRANDMOTHER
IN THE GORGIOLANDS

Sarah Wimbush is a Leeds poet who hails from Doncaster. Her debut poetry pamphlet, *Bloodlines*, won the *Mslexia*/PBS Poetry Pamphlet Competition 2019. It was published in 2020 by Seren and shortlisted in the Michael Marks Awards. In 2020 she was a winner in The Poetry Business Book and Pamphlet Competition with *The Last Dinosaur in Doncaster*, published by Smith|Doorstop in 2021. Her poems have appeared in *Brittle Star*, *The Interpreter's House*, *The North*, *Stand*, and most recently in *Wagtail: The Roma Women's Poetry Anthology* published by *Butcher's Dog*. Several poems have been highly placed in a number of single poem competitions, including 1st prize in the *Mslexia*, 2nd in the Ledbury and 3rd in The Plough. She is a member of York Stanza and Doncaster Read 2 Write, and received a Northern Writers' Award in 2019. Her first book-length collection, *Shelling Peas with My Grandmother in the Gorgiolands*, was published by Bloodaxe in 2022.

SARAH WIMBUSH

Shelling Peas
with My Grandmother
in the Gorgiolands

BLOODAXE BOOKS

ISBN: 978 1 78037 616 5

First published 2022 by
Bloodaxe Books Ltd,
Eastburn,
South Park,
Hexham,
Northumberland NE46 1BS

www.bloodaxebooks.com
For further information about Bloodaxe titles
please visit our website and join our mailing list
or write to the above address for a catalogue.

Supported using public funding by
ARTS COUNCIL ENGLAND

Cover design: Neil Astley & Pamela Robertson-Pearce.

Printed in Great Britain by Bell & Bain Limited, Glasgow, Scotland, on
acid-free paper sourced from mills with FSC chain of custody certification.

for Claire and Jess

CONTENTS

II

I

House

The first time
I went into a house
there were so many rooms.

Each one so big.
Each one so high.
Each with a door.

And in the middle of them all,
planks leading up to a framed sky.

White Cottage

When you finally took a house, it was white.
That houseland house, that lane-end house;
walnut trees towering above the church,
a limewashed privy, the broken stool with a heart
carved through the middle. You drew squares
on the house with your fingertips
and in these spaces you would make new windows
and edge them with let-down curtains.
You fitted a kitchen with the chop and slice
of your hands, *here, here, and here*:
make-do cupboards; the side-of-the-road sink.
We ate boiled bacon there with cold potatoes
and quince. Sundays, you'd toast pikelets by the fire
and we'd disappear inside hide-and-seek afternoons.
We grew to understand marriage in that house;
its ingrained sweat, its banter,
the bullfrog trapped in the cellar. Silences.
Museum house. Haunted house.
Walnuts blackened in jam jars like mouse brains.
The sewing-machine docking its relentless hum.
Was it the wind that flipped your Royal Worcester
off the dresser? And your charm bracelet
jangling like horse-sorters' reins
the day you filled the priest-hole with barrows of sand
and silenced that bastard frog.
You lost your flicker of threads: those owl eyes,
your tongue relaxing its waspy lilt. The woman
who kept a fire from New Year to Old Year's Day,
who pulled her own teeth
who never possessed a watch
who didn't exist on paper, and yet, could recite the name
of every pea field she'd ever worked through.
You, stood by the door, waiting
for the Gypsies to come and take you home.

'Shelling Peas with My Grandmother in the Gorgiolands' (opposite page): *gorgio:* non-Gypsy/ Traveller; *bender:* tent; *jukels:* dogs; *vardo:* horse-drawn caravan; *chor:* take

Shelling Peas with My Grandmother in the Gorgiolands

Never be surprised what gorgios say. Never mention Daddy
    juggled pennies on the back of a donkey.
        Never explain that Liza married the son of a king,

or how Gentle Hugh received the Mons Star, posthumously.
    Don't point out the in-between places. Don't speak
        of your love for a deadwood fire, and pretty-wear,

and how bare-knuckle fighting is as much a part of who you are
    as something they call 'class'. Never tell anyone
        when the visions come, that you collect dead

women's earrings, that you have always been frightened of water,
    except during a thunderstorm, when you stand
        at the lane end and burn like a flame in a lantern.

Never smoke a pipe until you're at least ten and steer clear
  of them North Country folk with their hob-cobbled jib.
    Never go to the fields in your grubbers,

wear a skirt and change behind a tree, and never ever let the lass
    next to you pull peas quicker than you.
        Never kiss a lad – you'll get in the family way,

and never get in the family way unless he'll do a runner with you.
    After, he's to torch the bender, straw ticks, corrupt linen.
        Never allow jukels inside the vardo,

or boil shimmies with pudding cloths, or leave a wound to turn –
    rinse with your own water or bind in a spider's web.
        Never chor what does not belong to you, or God,

and you'll do well my girl, to be match and master both
    with your old fella. Always keep one boot on the ground,
        tell your children's children their blood names,

and if, one day, you're in the company of gorgios,
    mind when to leave the book of your mouth open,
        when to fold it into a crossed knife.

Mother Tongue

I

Dukker is to see
the future, or your fortune,
while *dik* (sounds like deek)

is the word for look
which in my Yorkshire lingo
would be 'gis a dek'.

Eye translates as yok,
while *yog* is fire – and a branch
is firewood or *kosh*.

II

The voice a wild *grai*
(rhymes with eye) – a lexicon
of *jib* in my mind

wandering the land
over centuries, arrived
flaming, restless, thinned –

word legerdemain,
those Anglo-Romani psalms:
'*cushti*'… '*trushni*'… '*tan*'.

grai: horse; *trushni:* basket; *tan:* place

III

King Esau stories
'gutter Gypsy poetry' –
a fine *mush* who'd *chor*

the earth to protect
the poorest – their Robin Hood.
Some said deviant

others said brother
(pal from the Romanes *phral*)
I say: our Father.

IV

And the Rom renowned
for his *Jowi Grey* – as far
north as the Blacklands

where coal is *vonga*
(can also be money) – or
Brit. crib: 'wonga'.

Gorgio means neither
deep ravine nor incessant
hunger. However…

mush: man; *chor:* take; *Rom:* Gypsy man; *Jowi Grey:* bacon and potato stew; *gorgio:* non
Gypsy/Traveller

15

Dukkering

It comes
as it will.

Day or night.
Awake. Asleep.

I squeeze my eyes,
press my ears,
purse my lips,

until it fades –
this grain of sand
in my crystal eye.

dukkering: fortune-telling/seeing the future

Carroty Kate

I am dressed in last night's campfire
and dead men's boots.
My hair is the colour of a thousand foxy hawkweeds
and I own one red skirt
and a navvy's tongue.

I get by dukkering at the next market place –
sheeps' trotters or a brass groat
as payment for the reading,
my kissi belt strapped tight
to my left thigh. Time was,

you would have slapped me in irons,
dragged me to York Tyburn in a hay cart sat on my coffin,
where I'd be dropped
from the Three-legged Mare –
just for being.

dukkering: fortune-telling/seeing the future; *kissi:* purse

Gran Violet Applies a Poultice

I know good health stays with the child
born under a rising moon

and the sting of a honey bee's bite
can be eased with pollen from a meadow's bloom

and toothache's gnaw held at bay
by chewing wild garlic or cloves

and a spoonful of honey and elderberry
wards off winter's snivelling colds.

I know a tincture of burdock root
clears scurvy, bad blood and poor complexions

and being bunged up is easily solved
by scrumping a handful of Victoria plums

and a cup of fresh juniper bark,
rolled and steeped, relieves weary bones

and dandelion sap or well-hung pork fat
works like magic on warts and moles.

I know witchbane nailed to the eaves
forfends crawlers and the evil eye

and when they hang me from the crooked tree
I may walk-on but I never shall die.

Gal

I pause by the yog's blooming furze,
twilight unfolding its flittermouse wing
till I close like a hand into a fist.
Tethered to the seasons –
winter's gub on my skin, our jib in my song,
the drums roll skywest beneath my heels.

Here, I take only what I need
from the borrowed earth, hold gorgios
in my needle's eye, ask no favours.
And yet, in times of want there is nothing
I will not steal – nothing I would not give
to kin or the hedge-mumper or the manless.

Woman to the master of the grai; mistress
of sheaves and the flame-eyed hare,
I tame my smouldering curls and my otter bite,
press on with the doors, yearning
for the atchin tans where trees nurse the sun,
the places with whispered names:
Hagg Lane, Misson Springs. The Garden

'Gal': *yog:* fire; *gub:* curse; *jib:* language; *drum:* road; *gorgio:* non-Gypsy/Traveller; *hedge-mumper:* tramp; *grai:* horse; *atchin tans:* stopping places

The Hedgehog's Tale

She said a true Gypsy
wears an earth-brown neckerchief
dotted with box patterns, so fine
it flows like air
through his wedding ring.

She said, a slope near a river
is the best place to find a spring;
dig a hole,
watch the sand settle –
careful as you fill the kettle.

She said, you can feel rain coming
by the weight of the wind
and good scran
is as close
as a hedgerow and a fine tree –

spikes wrapped in clay and baked
in a fire pit, sweet
as a chestnut
then ripped
to suck the pith and juice and squeak.

John Thomas

He is the chav of the mam, drowned in a river accident
like a paper boat on her maiden voyage. He is the son
of the fatha who lost the plot, brought to roam wi nowt
but a hip-flask n compass in his hedge-mumper pocket.

He has a grandmammy who can skin a cat wi one shpeal
of her tongue n wastes two penn'orth on his gooin school.
Sixteen and he's pushin Grandma in her wicker bath-chair
up Huntingdon town n back, then stands with his chap

in his hand n his back to the wall wi the girl next dooar.
And his fingers gets trapped in the housemaid's drawers.
And he does a bunk to Godmanchester hiring fair.
And he's with Lord George Sanger's Circus fouar year.

He's wi lass after lass posterint next town. He's the rum'un
wi two lassies ont go, hoistint Big Top n tekin it darhn.
He's on the reigns cartint bear cage to Attercliffe: nods off,
rolls off, watches the steel-rimmed wheels trim his loaf.

He's an odd-job man, a pot man, a fish man in Tickhill village.
He's at the Gypsy encampment; he's the talk o the pitch,
the flattie whose heart beats a rhythm for Lizzie, his lass.
He is a rag man, a scrap man, a ganger, a this-n-that man.

He's a div wi that fat gal overt chip shop in Worksop.
He's a good fo nowt old bloke arght on his ear int doghouse.
He's a returner, a sometimes earner, loves a beer,
a bet, his chavs, his wife. Loves flyin his kite.

hedge-mumper: tramp; *flyin his kite:* having flings with other women

Pitched early mornin' at encampment o' Gypsy king Esau Smith

Not the circuit of wheat-lined drums
between Lincoln, Doncaster and Hoyland,
but Black Patch, its slag heaps rolling out
before their wooden wheels like a sea of tar.
That place, Smethwick, was said to be
on the other side of the Black Country,
but Lizzie would say: *so weir did't blackness begin,*
n end, fo this is't blackist country as eva known.
Already the vardo's fruit carvings would be bruised
with dustings of pitted charcoal; the piebald, Plunk,
draped in a sooty horse rug; the little ones
playing with kin on the cinder mounds,
faces polished as any collier or sweep.
On his return, her man was bear-black –
from the peak of his trilby to the toes
in the holes of his boots – a hard day
carting furnace waste from Soho Foundry.
While Lizzie scoured the slack with her sisters,
Hannah and Cinderella, digging for treasure
through the scoriae; metallic gems, glass-chinks,
glossy vonga, the shushi poaching all afternoon,
the sun doused to the arc in a farrier's horseshoe.
And magic bloomed, like naphtha lamps
held high over the forges and smelt works –
time to eat by the yog, share the old songs –
smoke Black Twist in clay pipes, liquorish ribbons
spiralling into throat-tightening bitterness,
the darkness beyond littered with diamonds.

vardo: horse-drawn caravan; *vonga:* coal; *shushi:* rabbit; *yog:* fire

Scrapping at Marshall's Engineering, Gainsborough

The big iron gates. Marshall's head man,
dead boilers laid out in the sun
like growing lads or six trombones
from marching bands, manhandled up
onto the dray. A mug of ale,
or two, at The Ferry Boat Inn
then back to the day's atchin tan

where rocks and jemmies batter steel
and brass apart. And by nightfall,
the hornet's nest of soot and scale
fades back to black; metals muscled
flat under saddles, bed bunks, hats,
until the price is right and just –
the's allus another war, lass.

Then to the scrappers, where the mash
is graded pure to fair to poor.
Weighed and bargained for. Collarless,
but waist-coated, each man commands
time on the floor: the not enough,
the puff and pout, hands open, slapped.
These men who live by wiser rules.
Outsiders. Set apart. Kings in fact.

atchin tan: stopping place

and lady housekeeper standing at the servants' entrance
and the onion sacks filled with steel pans, rabbit skins, cast-offs,
and the two wide skirts belonging old Lady Scarbrough.

And Daddy doffs his trilby, grease stains around the rim,
like a posh mush in his best gorgio: *thank you, dear Madam.*
And when it rains it rains and we sit it out beneath the dray,

and after several days the rags are dry, and the two wide skirts
go to Black Jess, the Maltby washer lass. And Daddy makes a bob.
And Jess swaps her old fella's hobnail boots for an orange.

mush: man; *gorgio:* non Gypsy/Traveller

Them Dunstan Kids

At the bend three boys
in black button-boots throw
stones, shout *Gyppos! Gyppos!*
Tommy knew their dad.

Further on, he stands the pony
in Scrooby mill-stream,
soaks the dray's squeaky wheel.
Along the lanes he thinks of that.

Our Jud

Sometimes he dug the ditches out on Serlby Hall Estate.
And thrashed his sister's man after he'd slapped her 'cross the face.
And often carried water for his mother from the Ouse.
And thieved ten shilling Great War pension off his brother Hugh.
And sang like an angel and played grass like a tin whistle.
And rarely missed a fisticuffing down the Old Blue Bell.
And that time calmed the lady's filly bolting up the road.
And couldn't write his name but nose-to-tailed a bookies board.
And got away with it that night those skewbalds went amiss.
And took a fair old beating 'cause he loved the married lass.
And didn't give a monkey's or ailed one day in his life.
And always wanted chavvies but never fancied a wife.
First to rise for threshing, last in a cock-fighting wager,
the man named after kings and coins and a dragon slayer.

chavvies: children

'Threshin'" (opposite page): *bender:* tent

Threshin'

On stubbled dust, field-workers gather
by newfangled machines; firebox stoked,
boiler banging hot to blanch and bubble

a clutch of corncrake eggs gleaned by Sam –
still warm from their bed of hay, chopped
on rough-grained bread and shared.

The lads hayfork stooks onto the stage
to feed the spinning drum, where it is said,
men have been dragged and eaten

up to their waists. Here, my sister Liza
(the day's band cutter on a man's wage)
cuts the twine and downs the sheaves

while our smallest take root on banks
with grandmothers, twisting gold into hats
and hearts and corn dollies. At one point

the thresher is stalled, to unpick a worm
of binder twine burrowed inside the straw.
Stoppage: uses light, loses brass –

but spoiled bedding can fell a beast if eaten.
I'm to keep the chaff hole clear where bract
is winnowed off the ears, and whooped

from the machine; chaff dust, hellish stuff –
bristles inside my headscarf, my shirt,
those moist places. Under florid skies

us girls jump into Scrooby pools,
scrub with willow sprays then return
to the pitch arm in arm,

to rest inside the bender night
to share a scrag end of ham and tatts –
the earth still warm as the air turns cold.

Straw Ticks

Threshing done,
Violet unpicks each straw tick
at one end
and dumps the dross onto the dray.

She scrubs the sacks
in a tin bath
with laundry soda and lavender
to fend off bugs,

then turns them on a hedge
while the lads cart the waste
to Goodall's yard
and feed it to the hogs.

Back at the patch
Hannah blends chopped straw
with rush and chaff,
and refills the ticks.

Under a tilting sun
the families gather and stitch the ends together.
And no one sleeps
till every bed is made.

Bedsheet

Take a bedsheet
with a hole in it.

Cut along the split.
Reverse, and stitch

the two good halves
together. Tuck over

a straw tick, until
another hole appears.

Divide again and sew
a pillowcase, or two.

And when they wear
see-through,

take each best face
and cut again

into poaching cloths
for puddings

or double-up
as nappies for the babies.

And from the scraps
make yourself a handkerchief.

Meat Puddin'

Take shin, kidney, an onion. Dice.
Cradle beef suet in your palm; shred
into flour with Daddy's shushi knife
lace-edged with rust. Add spring water.
Pullt goo into a ball.

Roll a circle with a besom end.
Scoop the mas and press onto the dough.
Gather like a pack-up. Flute the rim
with a lick of ale to seal together.
Gi the dumplin' skin a slap.

Turn onto a floured pudding cloth.
Tie a double knot. Slide into the cauldron
water thrilling over scavenged vonga,
one eye on the blip-blip-shudder till dusk.
Lift puddin' arht b't knot. Untie.

Ease the moon into an Imari bowl
haggled to a farthing from Black's pot barrow
on Retford market. Cut into a clock.
Add cooking liquor and salt –
n' then lass, eat wi carrots, tatties, swede.

shushi: rabbit; *mas:* meat; *vonga:* coal

Laneham Ferry

Cook roasts jugged hare
in the range at the Manor House.

Horse-drawn carts drive malt sacks
from a barge to the maltkins –

up the track past The Ferry Boat Inn
full of travellers drinking mead from tankards.

Past the Norman church and flood markers.
Past the sluice gates and along the byway.

Back at the landing stage
Robert Glossop winds the ferry boat in.

Folk make their way down the gangway;
load beasts, goods, horses. Pay the toll.

The rope eels through the water
looped over a pulley fixed at land's end.

In a minute, Robert will wind the ferry boat
across the Trent to Gainsborough.

The leaflet says: walk gets muddy in wet weather.
Not suitable for pushchairs.

The Bittern

After the glut of soft fruits,
and oat cakes toasting on the griddle,
and the deluge of Cox's,

it's the wintering-over
in two-up two-down cottage,
vardos stored on Big Frank's piece,

a squall of pheasant and quail
bartered for a tail-end of hogget,
mother schooling us by the range:

how to baste the skin to gold,
how to skim the fat for rushlights
and axels, how to eke the meat out

from pink to grey to dry; scraps
for soups, bones coddled to slate
in washday broth. All cushti scran.

And the hardness of spring.
Bitterns nesting in reed beds,
sweeter than heron –

the male's deep *whoohu-whoohu*
like a breath blown over a bottle.
On a still day, I feel that call for miles.

vardo: horse-drawn caravan; *cushti scran:* good food

The Calling Basket

Black velvet trim for mourning mantles are long-tails.
Mother-of-pearl buttons are a pair of lost souls.
Tapes, bindings and cord are pegs honed from hazel rods
sewn into the pleats and seams of ladies' bodices.
Elastics are willow girders for pants and drawers.
Nottingham lace is the pacing green at Thorne horse fair.
Threads are exotic birds from the Indian subcontinent
or a front parlour in Rossington. Broderie anglaise
is filigree cast in a foundry. This Old Holborn tin
is a bow-top wagon: acorn thimbles, ratter's teeth clasps,
press-snap hail; hooks and eyelets are twigs and leaves.
Needles are hob nails. Cotton reels are vardo wheels.
Ribbons are smoke signals for missies' pig-tails and china throats.
Centuries on the doors as queens of the Underworld.
Centuries walking the lanes as dust: a cup of tea in the desert,
read the leaves. The kindness of last year's bib and tuck –
thank ya kindly lady, yous be lucky. And gorgios
who hide behind lock and book and jacquard curtain –
this young monisher who buys a bud of lace,
her rush to cross my palm with brass.

long-tail: rat; *vardo:* horse-drawn caravan; *gorgio:* non-Gypsy/Traveller; *monisher:* woman

A Sund'y in Worksop

That morning, we pitch our caravans on Joe White's,
somewhere on Sime Street. Mother scrubs vardo floors
with washday waste, singing *Paddy McGinty's Goat* or maybe

I'll Take You Home Again, Kathleen. Daddy has a bloke to see
at The Old Ship Inn or perhaps The Robin Hood, God's people
blinking as they enter daylight. I stay with the tub cart

or was it the dray, water Plunk our dapple pony, or was it Spike
or was it Pluck? A school of men march into the yard, keen to win
a fortune with Pitch and Toss. From a corner the look-out boy

watches me. Beneath the sign, 'No Gambling Or Spitting',
the chuckers bless a fat penny each and bowl against the wall,
or could it have been into the air? Metals wield and thud.

Hoots and oaths. The men drift away, one lad left on the floor
or maybe leant against the wall, says over, *fot in't war, I did* –
and he has no hat. Or was it boots? Or was it both?

vardo: horse-drawn caravan

Late Afternoon by a Hedge

You insist on removing the black apron,
comb your fingers through those tangled curls.
I can see you pulling on your crocheted top,
the one it took two summers to make.
Your checked skirt seams are perfect. The mud
brushed away from your dancing shoes.

Hannah's arms hang from her shoulders
like dead rabbits, her face numb with fatigue.
But yours, yours tilts in defiance –
even when standing still you're moving.
You stare into the camera's blackness,
our eyes meet. Behind you there's a barn,

familiar, but then, I can't quite be sure.
The grass is long. Perhaps it's harvest time.
You buy a print from the travelling photographer.
Hannah sits by the campfire. You wrap
the crocheted top around the photograph.
Place it in your corner inside the vardo drawer.

vardo: horse-drawn caravan

Census 1911

On the census
Fanny is called Annie.
And head of the household, Thomas,
is born in Northampton, not London
and his occupation is flower hawker,
not scrap and rag dealer.

On the census, Annie (Fanny),
and young Tommy
are not learning to hawk
and trap small game, respectively –
they go to school.
And the family of nine are in renting
on Dock Road,

not travelling in vardos
through Laneham where Violet is born
on the side of the road
in a makeshift bender:
the bowed hazel and hessian sacks
fired after.

On the census,
Wife, Elizabeth, has no occupation,
although she will always be a pedlar,
and she is born in Doncaster, not Hoyland.
And Noah is their boarder,
not Elizabeth's brother.

On the census
Martha is thirteen
and the eldest of nine.
Not living in Worksop
with her grandparents
as an only child.

vardo: horse-drawn caravan; *bender:* tent

Earring

When they're young
pinch a lobe
until it's numb.

Place some bark
or apple skin
at the back,

thread a pin
and push the point
quickly in

and through.
Tie the thread
into a loop

like a ring.
Pull the cotton
now and then

to clear the hole
so the flesh doesn't grow
on the thread.

And when it's dry
take a knife
and cut the loop

then hang
a thick golden hoop.

The Ring

Imagine. Her hands snatching necks.
Shushi skins pinned into borrowed earth.
How she scrubs the gubbins from her garnet setting,
flogs the pelts to furriers for a bob or two.
That lift of soft fruit between finger and thumb.
Peas. Beans. How she buffs the harnesses in readiness
for Thorne Horse Fair – the Romani and Irish on the flash,
the open-lots and Burtons in a horseshoe around a yog –
fiddlers, jigs on boards, the clack-clack of spoons,
Jowi Grey on the wind, then spudding at Serlby.

Through fields, lanes, cobbled brooks:
posting rag-bills, hawking daffodils,
how she grips her lad's hand as they do a runner
to wed at Tinsley Church. And always that sense
of moving as one. The sky a hard master –
drums snug as an owd pair o chokkas,
carting castings at Steel Peech and Tozer
to Tickhill encampment hawking pots
to the hubbub of Black Patch mid-winter,
to those wide flat hayfields around Misson Springs.

How sometimes she only knows slack and air
and her wits – the atchin tans: Foundry Lane,
Great North Road, Gibbet Hill, Attercliffe.
No half-dead frills only her histories
and the seasons: the earlies, the hoe, wheat stooks,
mother's calling basket, wintering-over,
rabbit skins parched to stiff tambours.
Imagine this ring – my grandmother's ring.
Its Gypsy setting. Its golden eye burnished
with all the jib and ancients it has worn thin.
See, here on my finger. How it fits.

shushi: rabbit; *open-lot/Burton:* types of *vardo* (horse-drawn caravan); *yog:* fire; *Jowi Grey:*
bacon and potato stew; *chokkas:* boots/shoes; *atchin tans:* stopping places; *Gypsy setting:*
similar to a bevel ring setting

Walking Girl

I borrow the Earth
as I go on my journey –
burn only deadwood,
leave the nest half full.

Gorgios, you'll do well
to take heed of my story:
we are guests in this Kingdom,
architects of our Road.

gorgio: non-Gypsy Traveller

The Astronaut Who Came to Tea

Theirs was a strange spacesuit.
Some wore garb the colour
of saffron, pimpernels, dirt-tracks,
girded themselves with sovereign
coinage and jaunty brims. Others
swashed skin plump as horse-
chestnuts launched from bowed hulls.
We'd haggle cobs and hoofwork
at the market, had our wickerings
repaired, our foibles sharpened.
They bought our milkmeatbread,
bewitched us with sorcery
and fiddlejigs: that intergalactic cant,
and every year an Astronaut
worked the doors, and my mother
would invite her in to tea.
I recall the gravitational pull
of fire-scars and bracts,
how the visitor promised her people
come lay the hawthorn
a nod being her word.
Mother picked moonbow ribbon
from the trushni for my hair
while the Astronaut would sip
from a china cup, swirl it,
and stare into the leaves.
Something was sometimes said,
sometimes not. She'd walk-on
with a pillowcase of East India tins,
lesser linen, rags, and gave my
mother *cushti bok* which she clung
onto. Once, I crept down
to the shuttles, the Nauts orbiting
their yogs like bats and hidden
deep inside the black hole
of the copse I could taste
the liberty, and a cosmic particle
inside me would ache.

Then one year the landings flooded
with red brick and privet
and the space people didn't come,
and the next year, till they were gone
and someone said, if they did return,
livestock would disappear
and Lord help the women –
so we edged our blades, built wall
upon wall,
              and new skywalkers
lug the back-breakery.
They land every June.
Light years away from kin
they sleep in metal cabins
chained to Earth, and exist
to harvest our neat sweet greens.
I saw her the other day,
the Astronaut who came to tea,
stood on the edge of Common Street,
woollen shawl lifting
as the juggernauts roared past,
face pinched to a dried-out chestnut –
her lunar gaze, all that dark matter.

trushni: calling-basket; *yog:* fire; *cushti bok:* good luck

In the Library

I stop-start on my journey along the multicoloured shelves,
pull out three books. The black and white man

pushes past; his arms swish-swishing like swords,
his palms damp with newspaper print.

My granddaughter and I sit at the reading table.
We have lived through every circle in the English oak.

I read to her from the Bible, and then *To Kill a Mockingbird*.
The black and white man blows his nose. Everyone looks up.

He marches past us: bigger, fatter. Blacker. Whiter.
Something flutters from his pocket to the floor.

My granddaughter runs across, picks up his library card,
holds it out to him. He takes it with a smile.

Back on my lap her blonde hair is rue and wood smoke.
I open *We Are the Romani People* and read to her.

Gifts

(after David Morley's 'Lyrebirds')

You gift the gray's tone. A gold sovereign placed on one eye.
    I discover a swell of heather, the jay's blue, the wide wide dawn.

You gift Lyrebirds' wings; pegged-out washing snagged on a thorn.
    I discover the pitch of a mer-Rom's perfect note across the May.

You gift a scar from a cut-throat razor sliced across a page.
    I discover waveform; a war cry, a red feather, the Novra runes.

You gift the gift of speckled eggs, the clack of freshwater stones.
    I discover a lynchpin and trig point inside the mizzling cape.

You gift reed warblers perched on candelabras in the mist.
    I discover woods, words, a sword of spells bunched up on a larch.

You gift a duty clip around the ear from a kindling star.
    I discover the warmth of Salt Szek as she wanders past.

You gift pirri-pirri burrs pinned into my diction's northern crest,
    you gift this: a whisker from the oldest wolf in the forest.

Bloodlines

In the Bloodlines
there's a hooped earring.
In the Bloodlines there's an open vardo
door, ramsons on the other side. Songs and seasons
wave at you from the Bloodlines, atchin tans watch you
fly. In the Bloodlines there's an acorn of swagger that
inflates into a barrel wearing a vest. In the Bloodlines
there is nothing to offer up to the Old World except
a pair of shammy bootees –
your past, their past.
Bloodlines stare,
bemused by the
chant of Tables,
a company car;
lunch. Bloodlines
hoick slingshots at
woodcock and snipe.
Damp earth is a must
as you lie with the Bloodlines,
some scratch the name of the wind into elm with a crotchet hook,
others chor lollipops from children. Bloodlines can't hear you but
they follow you in a handful of photographs and crumpled vowels:
the shortening clay pipe; *gorgio fowki*. In the Bloodlines you make
yourself make steamed pudding, then eat salad. In the Bloodlines
there's a long blue thread. In the lea and the lanes there must be
someone who can tell you about the Bloodlines; about
the rhythm of your tongue, your flying fox glare,
the need to set curtains ajar at night.
What are you searching for
in the darkness? Why are you?
And yet, it's the Bloodlines
that murmur on the barval,
Bloodlines that understand
the spell of a campfire,
your attraction to gold,
how if I shuck my paleface
from gullet to hairline,
the world would turn
scarlet and all that pours
out will be road.

44

II

'Bloodlines' (opposite page): *vardo:* horse-drawn caravan; *atchin tans:* stopping places; *chor:* take; *gorgio fowki:* non-Gypsy/Traveller folk; *barval:* wind

Pilgrim Queens

Some brought thread, spindles, bodkins and intrepid hearts.
Some wore coifs and doublets with petticoats over gowns.

Some brought acorns to scatter with washerwoman's hands.
Some wore the roll of the ocean with sea-legs; some did not.

Some brought willow bark, feverfew, dried lion's tooth.
Some wore scant comfort. Some wore the careless cough.

Some brought oiled paper for windows, bolster pillows, dogs.
Some wore the flame of a matriarch; some were mice, some shrews.

Some brought rags and worked scraps into squares to patch quilts.
Some wore wonder at marlin drawn to the hull.

Some brought hard-headed children: *Remember, Resolved, Love.*
Some wore blather, others brought hornbook and quill.

Some wore the fury of death with a psalm, some a grimace.
All brought God's Word in a box to a hopeful place.

Things My Mother Taught Me

So, know how to recognise a female brown crab?
Hens are by far the juiciest and most delicious, naturally.
Cock crabmeat leaves a slight aftertaste, like ammonia
Mum would say. And a bacon sandwich is best cut
with dress-making scissors, and if you see black steak
in the reduced section at Morrisons, buy it quick –
except pork with a rainbow glaze, avoid that like the plague.

A spoonful of sugar or cake helps a fire to catch
and wrapping paper can be re-used at Christmas
and birthdays by removing the sticky tape –
forget the scars, no one would dare to complain.
Leftover Dulux mixed together makes interesting wall colour,
and the best thing to feed kids after swimming is pancakes;
first with orange, then treacle if you have it, or sugar.

A pair of pants on top of your tights (as well as underneath)
keeps them up all day and a silly green bobble hat will
stop you catching that cold, and washing-up liquid cleans the bath
almost as well as Ajax but without the itchy residue. Never
cross on the stairs, nor touch wood, or open an umbrella indoors,
and if Copydex turns to rubber in the middle of a school project
flour and water is a good stopgap, even with the lumps.

On Doncaster Market you can buy crab in all sorts of ways;
brown paste, arm-and-a-leg white meat, or a hotchpotch of both.
Or from regiments of ceramic croissants with pie-crust edges,
boiled into pink oblivion next to the uncooked; wide-eyed
and numb on their bed of ice. Antennae twitching. Touching.
Males have pointed bellies and by far the larger claws, whereas
the female has broader shoulders, her heart pinned to her chest.

Inside Lingerie

It's a phenomenon every woman knows well – the entrance
to Debenhams or Marks and Spencer's *Bra Fitting Department*,
where men of a certain age congregate on Sunday mornings.

There's the one who sits, cross-legged on a velour tub chair,
so compelled by yesterday's cricket score in the *Evening Post*
that you have to walk around him;

the one who stares into space, shop lights twinkling on his brow
and the one who stands with the bags, taking the measure of each woman
as she enters and leaves, wondering – *just what exactly goes on in there?*

And the husband who stands poker-straight, arms folded,
next to the scarlet push-me-up JJ cups.
Like his flaming bus is never going to come.

2:15 at Doncaster

I see them, there, on the turf
mingling with the top hats and touts,
jockeys' silks, the roustabouts in neckerchiefs.
I spotted him immediately –
the wince in that listing gait,
his pelvis smashed beneath a bank of coal.
His daughter walks beside him
dark and slender in the purple dress.
I peer into the black and white screen –
Mum, can you see me?

Piggott is in the paddock.
My grandmother has ten bob on his nag's nose,
talks *form* as she nips her cigarette
then thrums a hem into my new red skirt
cut from the back of her old coat.
And they're off.
I wander outside
pick the last caterpillars off sprout-tops for Gran,
spend an hour swinging on a tyre.

When voices spill out of the house
I run back in, scooped up by callused hands,
press my face into Grandad's neck;
stubble, stale tobacco, the warmth
of sure-things and a rank outsider.
It's dark before I even realise –
the St Leger *is* the end of summer.
I can't take my eyes off these people,
reduced to almost nothing, then returned
somehow bigger and more real.

The Pencil Sharpener

Fridays were pencil sharpening.
Like a bus conductor's ticket machine
clamped on the teacher's desk –
that squeeze to uncurtain the cavity,
insert a stub, then turn the lever with a whirr
until out came a skin-fresh pencil,
pastry skirt, the point a tack;
all the pencils in the pot
uniform-striped red and black.

Our pencils were oddments drawn
from Argos and Mum's work. Spelling nights

Dad would shear the carving knife
with a steel: once, twice, a third
to set the edge, then slicing forwards
peel a pencil like a pear. He'd blow
the ice-pick tip and jab his thumb
to test for firmness, then
above the whiteness he'd excite the air
with tiny circles. I imagined words
like: daughter, sharpen, write.

Giant Leaping

You should have been an astronaut. When I was young
you spent Saturday afternoons watching Formula 1
curtains drawn, in the front room, like James T. Kirk
sat in your chair, dodging asteroids and black holes,
drawn into the glare of the black and white set;
driving at warp speed into outer space. At the age of eight
I left the bike outside the shop, and when it got nicked
you scratched your head with a pencil
as if you were trying to fathom some astrophysical equation,
but you didn't bollock me, all that much.
And when I was ten you came back from the tip
with a washing-machine door
and we used the glass for a goldfish bowl,
then a trifle dish. And when I was twelve,
you spent hours in the bathroom, in womb-like darkness
lifting our likeness from acid white trays,
then hung us out to dry on the shower rail.
By the time I was fourteen, you'd built a contraption
on the conservatory roof: an old door, silver foil,
a radiator, set at an angle to the other planet,
and if we turned the spanner in the tank cupboard
the water was glorious for at least two minutes.
And when I was married, you put our wardrobe together;
it took longer than expected, then later we found the fixings
we'd forgotten to give you, but you never said,
and it's still up there. And when you came to stay over
the echo of your voice rumbled, through the mortar
like a grumbling volcano, and the kids couldn't sleep
so I lay down with them absorbing the shock waves.
And today you're eighty. And the rim of your cap shines
where you lift it off, and you're still lopping logs with a chainsaw
like peas from a pod. And I bite my lip,
not sure I can suggest you put your feet up:
all men of weight struggle with that one small step.

I learned to drive in a metallic blue Ford Capri

I learned to drive in a metallic blue Ford Capri
Mk 1, J reg, high mileage, black leatherette upholstery.
I learned to drive in a metallic blue Ford Capri:
gloves in the glove compartment, dog on the parcel shelf,
five gears, two doors, four seats; ruptured exhaust gaskets
so them in the back suffered headaches
and breathing difficulties. I learned to drive
in a metallic blue Ford Capri, bit like Bodie and Doyle
or Starsky and Hutch even: rectangular head-lamps,
suitcase boot, twenty to the gallon, vinyl roof, bucket seats.
I learned to drive in a metallic blue Ford Capri

and Dad said, *if you can park that lass, you can park
anything*. And I can. I learnt to drive at sixteen
on a derelict runway: revs that screamed,
nine point turns, kangaroo hops, Dad's knuckles tighter
than wheel nuts as he yelled *you can gu faster
if ya like love*. And I did. Once, in poor judgement
and fading light I took out a lamppost,
so we fixed her, together: wet and dry, *The Express*,
masking tape, body filler ('mud' to him and me),
and a grey base paint washed with metallic blue waves.
Dad even let me spray. A bit. I used to drive
a metallic blue Ford Capri. Then, her big end fell off.

A rattle appeared. Rust nibbled her carcass.
And Dad said it was her time to go. Now, I'm no petrolhead
but if Wheeler Dealers brought her back from the dead
and I'd a few grand spare, I'd be there like a shot:
that yank of the choke, long deep throw of the gear stick,
the heave of the windows and non-powered steering,
the blow of the exhaust and click of the mileage,
the stink of the ashtrays, and the fish and chip Fridays.
I'd peddle the metal down the back road to Maltby,
elbow on the window, *Born to Run* on the cassette,
going faster, going farther, going for ever, nothing better –
'cause it's just not the same in a white Ford Fiesta.

Visiting My Aunt on Her Birthday, 1st September 1979

We lick our fingers and dot
hundreds and thousands off the melamine plate.

The radio beeps with The News.
Jean and Mum fall silent –
Barbara Leach is added to the list.

Don wanders in with fragments of bone
from the border, probably a cat,
his Sunderland twang.

Interviewed by West Yorkshire Police.
Handwriting that didn't match. Twice.

13.11.20

Uncle Reg

had two Gloucester Old Spots named Reggie and Violet,
bantams in the kitchen, three fingers on one hand,
and an earth closet you could see all the poo and wee in.

He loved my grandmother even though he'd just been the lodger.
Years after, I'd receive a £1 Premium Bond on my birthday,
all of which I still have, but none of the millions hoped for.

Teatimes, I'd watch him scurry about like Alice's rabbit,
then later, drowsing in the collapsing chair, he'd rest the metal
of his pocket watch against those two unlucky stumps.

Between *Mary Berry's Baking Bible* and *My Class Enjoys Cooking*

there's *Modern Practical Cookery*.
Rebound with Bero paste and bedsheet ribbons,
you relax on the eBay table,
glad of the rest from all that standing.

Unused for years but read, shelved, read,
you remain on the kitchen shelf.
Each splodge, each blown stain
amber on your frosted cover –

pages so brittle, if I let you slip
you would smash across the tiled floor:
Contents, *Hors D'oeuvres*,
Empire Recipes; *Woman's Own* snippings –

orange sellotape unsticking cuttings,
paper thinned from a million finger turns:
Tripe and Onions, Semolina Soup,
Christmas card bookmarks,

a paper rose, marginalia: 'my curry'.
Each time, you bustle in reeking
of a thousand crumbles, gingham housecoat,
bombs, birthdays, talc. Kisses.

Rebel

Pangrams and ASCII Art

I'm not sure who suggested Typing.
I do remember it being thought of as an essential skill
for a girl lacking academic potential.
Perhaps that was why I always let myself down:
unable to reach forty words per minute
let alone sixty, hopeless at sitting
with feet flat, one leg slightly forward.
I can hear Miss Finley now – *correct positions!*
glaring at me over the Sherman Imperial.
If I could have concentrated I'm sure
I would have remembered *Dear Mr Jones*
closed with *sincerely* not *faithfully*,
(particularly the small s), I'd have sent
'the quick brown fox jumping over that flaming lazy dog'
rather than a crazy frog, and possibly
enjoyed Christmas cards 'for fun'.
All those Xs in agonising alignment:
a snowman, or a cute reindeer
or a spruce tree decorated with red O baubles
– that's O as in Oh! not 0 as in zero.
Mine always looked like a game of Jacks
or a machine gun attack, and I can tell you now,
in fact I'm sure Miss Finley knew,
I typed Rudolph's nose with a capital R.
In black. On purpose.

A Spring Morning

You crouch in the daffodils
digging for treasure
with your little trowel.

I spin the ball past Ruby
then glance across,
you holding up the sticky entrails
swirling them like gum

where moments before
the fat stump of a worm
had inched across your palm.

Vixen

I wait outside my daughter's boyfriend's house.
Ignition off. Radio low.
I rarely feel my hackles rise
at my desk, or in Tescos, but here

a flicker creeps into my peripheral vision –
fire on black – a comet's trail, then
a head that oscillates; her upturned snout.
I switch the radio off. Watch from above.

She paws the tarmac, bows to me – but no,
slides her jaws around a roadkill squirrel,
its compressed plume tail.
Slinks off to where the foxes go.

Pompocali

I'd like to bring you here
to these random mounds on the edge of the woods,
sandy paths
gouged by bike
and boot and dog, wind tugging madly at the heather.

Me being me,
I like to imagine an Empress buried deep inside,
a Roman coin
placed on her tongue,
jade pendant resting on her first rib,

bones still wrapped
in scraps of silk, the hint of rose water – *'per fumum'*.
But as we reach the plateau
I'd have to explain
that these mounds are in truth, slurry, grit, gobs of clay

dumped beside a brook
where stone was quarried by crack of tongue and whip
to build fortress towns
like Eboracum or Danum,
rivulets feeding into the stream –

an ancient watering place for bear and wolf
or cupped in the hands
of Celtic Britons,
or indeed a slave's
taking back her freedom after the Empire's collapse –

home the wildlands of Petra or Namibia,
her heartbeat faster than the startled doe's
as it stumbles across my path
where our eyes meet,
and for a moment, I forget that you're not here.

Pompocali: Mounds in Hetchell Woods near Leeds, thought to be spoil heaps
from Roman earth-workings.

Trip to the National Portrait Gallery, with the wife

We started at some strange names, van Eyck,
Arnolfini, then the face of Henry the Eighth,
I recognised him. It was at the line engraving
of A Tudor Lady that I turned off, and leaned against a door,
chewing a speck of muck from under my thumbnail.
Trying to hurry you past Cromwell, I noticed the faces
becoming more realistic, warts and all, and as I waited

by Rembrandt by Rembrandt, a bloke stared at me
from across the room. We moved into the 19th Century
where you spent what seemed like eternity
with the Brontë Sisters, your face flush. *Just look at them!*
I looked, saw nothing, except a dull painting
of three old-fashioned women scored with a cross,
as if it had once been folded like an England flag

or a tablecloth. He was there again, on the other side
in his tight red T-shirt, staring. By Robert Stephenson
I'd begun to run out of steam and at Queen Victoria,
my patience. I sighed, hoping you'd get the message,
and as you glanced up with that exuberant grin, I felt him
beside me. After Oscar Wilde (Men of the Day No.305)
we paused, and I sat on the long cool bench

in front of General Officers of World War I. All those faces
staring out… and for the first time, I wondered,
what happened to them, these khaki-clad cocksure men?
He sat beside me, the creases in his jeans puckering up,
an almost agreeable space between us, and then
that uneasy feeling, like when someone knows
what you're thinking. And a hint of musk…

Sod Lowry and Freud, I was getting out of there.
What about David Bowie? Next time, I told you – I nearly ran
down the steps. Disappointing to leave so soon love,
I know, but you can't have everything in life. Looking back
across St Martin's Place, he was stood
in the museum entrance; man bag strapped across his chest,
thumb in his Levi's, a gorgeous smile on his face.

The Powder-monkey's Apprentice

Mostly, it comes during the night.
Gnaws at me till I grab my jeans,
tiptoe downstairs through the smoke
kissing the creaks, then pad out onto snow.
Other times, it's a stone-breaker's yard.
I wasn't ready for it in the beginning;
the flail of a silent disco, the spew,
but recently it has crystallised into polar bears
roasting on coals; Vikings, harvest mice,
knapweed; space dust, and a fine tree
in a mast year bombarding me with oaknuts.
It even played-out like Sid once, and I pogoed
up to the last fake cord in *God Save The Queen*.
When I finally understood what it was –
a tall woman with hair the colour of sulphur
stood on the top deck of the last bus to Wakefield
shouting, *yes, yes, YES!* –
I knew it would always be part of me.
I'd had to die to realise that it was part of me.
Now, I wear the purple dress with the red hat
and my eyes are a bull shark's, peeled
and oiled, waiting for the slightest chink.
It roller-blades through me on hot Sunday afternoons
waxing in Old Norse and Seamcrawler,
or rokkers Romanes as I circle
like a red kite over ancient woodland,
hounded by hooded crows, me flicking my V tail.
But however it comes, I know it will never love me.
I know heroin dressed as a lost child's stare.
Still, I take the whole of it inside me,
gulping and swelling till I am a city:
the tsunami walls; a rare moth fluttering past –
these things that hunt us down like roadkill,
saltpetre or apple blossom, to emerge black
and scratchy and with something to say.

rokkers: talks

Peasholm Park

Aunty Ann skips down the path, at double speed.
She's wearing a grey flower-power dress
in fact, the whole park is monochrome –
the grass, the dragon boats. Uncle John waves
from Grandad's shoulders, same cheeky grins.

Mum is sitting on a picnic rug, ankles crossed.
Like Bridget Bardot she leans back and laughs
in mute; the picture hangs, reels in, and in,
till it's a close-up: doe eyes, porcelain skin.
Sixty frames per second and it's a photo shoot –

she's a David Bailey smiling directly at me.
A sea breeze blows a lock of hair across her face
and with a delayed blink, she pushes it away,
an astronaut with Barbarella fingers. Pouts.
I'm as young as my daughter, hair thinner than Dad's

on Nan's knee in a deckchair she'll never get out of.
Same boiled eggs, same cornet mitten,
except the rug is technicolor tartan with a plate
of real meat sandwiches. Nan spits on a hanky
and scrubs my toothless grin. White screen.

Blood Sugar

Dear Jenna. Even though I'm at that age where I'd rather forget birthdays, I was excited to receive *Museum of Ice Cream* as a gift from a friend who'd heard me mention it, you and I having been on that course together, where I realised that we have common ground on more than one subject, so I sat down to read it immediately because it was my birthday, and on your birthday you can do anything you like, well, almost anything that's legal, like reading a book on a Saturday afternoon, even though you should be digging up weeds, or clearing out the fruit bowl, only to find myself instantly thrown by the missing dash in *Ice Cream*, and the fact that there was no picture of ice, or cream, or ice-cream on the cover, just half a satsuma with its exposed pith, and the more I thought about it, the more *Ice Cream* sounded like I SCREAM, but I carried on, because of the weird taste of any sweet-flavoured cream, iced or not, wanting to know how a seaside 'treat' could become an institution, hopeful that no one else had ever wondered about the weirdness too, and I read the collection twice, without breathing, from the first poem to the last simulation, each page melting between my fingers, not the kind of melt I'd experienced when my oldest friend disappeared before my eyes, and my heart split like the over-ripe orange I dropped on her cream carpet, that melt was different; me apologetic trying to dab it out, first unsuccessfully with a tissue, then scrubbing it with Persil on a scourer turning the stain brown, although by that point she didn't care about the stain, or her overgrown garden, or her birthday – no, it was more the kind of melt you feel when you see a car shadowing a bike, or you can't take your eyes off the single swaying elephant in a zoo, which reminds you of the 99 gripped in your hand as a child, you not knowing what to do with it, especially the flake, unable to throw it to the ground, not because it was a treat, or because the family lapped theirs up like whiskery old dogs, it was more the insidious sweetness of it, the slavering over your fist, the way it crawled down the stick of your arm, while minor planets dripped from your elbow onto the golden sand below in small black dots.

William Shaw is lowered down the shaft

The water below has its own devices.
Above, the pit mouth wanes into a moon.
I stretch, I reach out into darkness

to secure the clamp and in the twist
I lose my grasp on the sinking tool.
The water below has its own devices.

Silence, then a splash from the abyss.
My footing slips, and like a fool
I stretch, reaching out into darkness,

tumbling from the hoppit's abrupt list
into the belly of a black lagoon.
The water below has its own devices.

A chill gathers in the blackness;
the muddy wall, its inexorable cocoon.
Stretching, I reach out into darkness.

The pit mouth begins to evanesce,
my lungs tightening balloons.
The water below has its own devices –
I stretch, I reach out into darkness.

hoppit: large metal bucket used to transport men and materials during the sinking
of a pit-shaft

Hillards

In the doorway next to Hillards there's a man.
In the doorway next to Hillards there's a man and a dog.
A man and a dog and a cardboard box.
A man, a dog, and a cardboard box, and the people
are walking past the doorway next to Hillards.
Past the man who's been on the edge
for almost a year, a man with a collie on a rope.
The dog watching people walk past –
that weird blue eye. And the dead cigarette
wedged between the man's index and middle finger,
like a salute; reminding himself who he is,
as he stands in the doorway next to Hillards.
It isn't a Walkers' crisps box, no it's smaller,
like it once held something sweet
like bags of toffees or plums, as he dreams of notes
but would be glad if loose change
or a tin of tomato soup drops into the box
as he disappears in the doorway next to Hillards.
The flap on the box has something written on it.
Words that started out bold and black
then fade away as the ink ran out, and the nib
had to scratch, Miners, in 'Support The Miners',
as he took off his parka and told the collie to sit
and stood in a shop doorway with nothing left,
then nipped his smoke and dug a message
of hope into corrugated card, and stroked his dog
while they wait in a doorway for us to stop
and put coppers or tins into a cardboard box.
Next to Hillards. The supermarket that was.

STOP!

It starts with hearts. Red and broken on a soapbox behind a criss-cross
of barbed wire. We pull up a car tyre, drag shop fittings out of a ditch,

throw on sapling oaks, half a besom, unhinge a litter bin. The village
comes out in support, donates a lion's roar and a bedstead in case of a nifty kip,

and more: an oil drum and a strip-a-gram for entertainment; skinny roll-ups,
and chips and scraps for snap; Welly lock-ins and two football teams

to keep us sane. Mothers bolster us with pit props and builder's brew –
housecoat grenades. A window cleaner gifts his ladder for a quick escape.

All anchored down with women's tights and washing line, and yet, we wonder
how far do powder-monkeys and rippers have to go to save their jobs?

Still, we stand firm on the wooden plank. We are stoked, and black
and white, young and old; eye to eye and pole to pole beside the winding gear.

This barricade is our pyramid; our eagle's nest on Everest, our stage.
They beckon from afar *call it time, lads*. We show a sign, we have our say.

Welly: Miners' Welfare Club

Rosso Youthy 1984

Talk's all pit-head gates:

men chasing men down Holmes Carr,
under washing-lines, through Mr Shaw's marigolds.

Two Tribes reverberates through plastic orange chairs
Angie and Dirty Den hard at it in the pool room.

Maureen hands out squash and *Sherbet Dip Dabs* –
food parcel hand-outs from the Welly soup kitchen

– kin' hell, di ya clock Stig's old man knock that bobby's lid off!

The amber of a cigarette, a finger held aloft
passed around like a syringe full of shit,
drawn into a tail of drooping ash.

Each son careful not to be the one
to let it   break   away.

Welly: Miners' Welfare Club

Near Extinction

I

No otters in the River Don.
No rest for Sylvia Grant-Dalton
upholding Brodsworth Hall: subsidence
scribbled on the wall –
the roof a drain, gardens besieged.
A losing battle.

Down the lane, Brian
at Brodsworth pit
with his mullet and denim jacket:
windswept, sun-kissed – convinced
they can turn the tide
in landlocked South Yorkshire.

II

Rossington. *Like Beirut*,
says Mrs Selby, watching ghosts
of picket line past –
burned-out cars,
burned-out hearts.
Mr Selby in his chair, waiting
for the snowdrops.

An action shot of Lesley Boulton:
camera in hand, the raised baton –
a pin-up girl at Highfields Welfare.
Wives on battle stations
in the soup kitchen.
Men fed first.

III

Outside the new Frenchgate Centre –
a band of brothers riddled with badges,
rattle buckets – 'Miners Children's Xmas Party'
all around the world turned
outside in.

Paul, just nineteen, marching back
with the shift and his Grandad
to Markham Main: end of the line,
final man down, under that headgear –
the last dinosaur in Doncaster.

Markham Main

Afternoons, they meet up
on street corners
like old youths planning revolution.

Gaffers, fathers, brothers –
an hour at the Club with a pint.
Go over the end again, and again.

How they were the last by three days
to stay out in Yorkshire.
How they'd *gu back tomorra*.

After school, they take the grand-kids
to the Pit Top Playground, look forward
to the night shift at IKEA. Together.

The York, Edlington

Opposite what was the Manager's house
and next to the old Junior School –
the haunt of floorboards creaking
under the early shift's pit boots.
Chaplin eyes follow ale up to the rim,
Harry's whispers in the barmaid's hair,
her intoxicating laugh, her skin.
The clean taste of bitter, the hush
of a domino game. Outside, a blue
electric sign above the door: *WOK ONE*

The Lost

At the unveiling of the restored Lovers statue
outside The Staff of Life, *All You Need Is Love*
playing on the tannoy, Margaret lingered once again –
the golden couple married at the pelvis, giant limbs
restructured, fibreglass skin resprayed...
                                        there was a time
Margaret wore rollers under her headscarf
at the pickled onion factory behind Ford of Britain,
her nan and mam over the other side of the Don
at Crompton Parkinsons, swapping radio batteries
for .303 rifle ammunition, then fluorescent tubes.
After her Friday shift, Brenda splashed out on cod
at Doncaster market served by Lesley
daubed in sky blue eyeshadow, *ya right ma love?*
Elsie's grand-kiddies scrubbed up nice
on Saturdays at Greyfriars Baths,
changing them in poolside cubicles,
all their worldly goods in one wire basket, her youngest
Wendy on overtime at Bridon Ropes,
their cables still lowering men down shafts –
that manriding accident at Bentley pit,
the seven lads who never came back – while at Peglers
Kevin Keegan began to make a name for himself.
And across Doncaster Carr the Travellers and Gypsies
pitched up with the wily hares and kingfisher flits,
while the filthy rich lorded-it in NCB's Coal House
and Plant apprentices escaped at snap time in packs;
young and fit and sweet with sweat and engine oil,
green overall sleeves tied around their waists
eyeing the typists on lunch breaks who breathed
into pencil skirts at Chelsea Girl, then a quick shop
at Hillards before they all clocked back on.
Town always chocka: buses stuck in traffic
Rovers playing Barnsley FC, or Leger week fair;
spinning waltzers and gobsmacked goldfish
or that airshow malarkey at Finningley.
Gooin' round Donny town Satdy? Lager,
lager and lime, lager and black, lager bitter,

Lambert and Butler, The White Bear,
The Old Volunteer, The Yorkist,
Main Line, King's Head, Nag's Head,
real ale at the Hallcross, real men in Beethams,
The Bistro for a friend of a friend's wedding,
brandy and Babycham on special occasions,
a curry at the Indus; *good evening ladies.*
And inside the Arndale an eighteen-year-old girl
waiting for her boyfriend beneath The Lovers –
like birds in a cage
water streaming down gilded wires
fingertips reaching for the sky.
How their fibreglass feet were shattered
by the lump hammer, how they were rocked
and ripped away by developers, then salvaged
for a backhander, and planted
like an autumn maple, in a garden, in Bessacarr
and forgotten,
                          till today, outside Waterdale:
limbs splayed, bodies still joined at the hip in an X
heads flung back, the sky grinding across them
and the model villages
and the churches selling carpets
and the factories turned call centres,
the school yards, the ginnels, the smokeless chimneys
and beneath them, beneath all that, those lost men,
and all that blackness still down there.

Our Language

This is the voice. This is the sound of the broad and gubbed, the Undermen; the too-young, the faced-up, the midnight-blue tattooed. These are mouths fit to bust with faultlines and deputy sticks, the crackling of airlocks, motties, cages and tubs; throats riddled with methane and headstocks, gob-stink and dog-ends, of nights and days and afters, and the short walk home as dawn spills over the tip at the end of the houses. This is the language of the pony riders and jumped-up checkweighmen, of Davy lamps and Dudleys, the oncostlads and gaffers, of black-nails and snap-tins, and names like Arthur passed down through time till it's more than a name, it has new meaning like the word GIANT or STONE. It is not dole-wallahs, nor the never-never, nor the light-fingered, nor more to be pitied than talked about, although talked about all the same, it is making your mark with a cross and having faith in what's beneath. It's friend-ship. It's *fuck the bastards*. This is the tune of haulage boys and shot-firers and Elvis impersonators, their legs smashed to bits at the bottom of shafts and the women who feed every-one's children. Sometimes the words speak for themselves at galas or picket lines, or not at all, on those rare rest days, by a well-stocked lake, where men of rock are silenced by a distant horizon. I could catch this language and write it out for those who want to know, I could place it in their palms to hold like a squab and watch it swell with all its 'boot rooms' and 'slack', because our language still exists. It roars by gas fires, and at the far table in the Club, and in the living museum beside the image of a man digging forever through a coal seam two foot thick. It is black lung and unwritten songs. It is soup kitchens, work vests, hewers. Picks.

ACKNOWLEDGEMENTS

Thanks to the editors of the following publications where some of these poems appeared: *Atrium, Brittle Star, Culture Matters, Dream Catcher, The Friday Poem, High Window, Ink Sweat and Tears, The Interpreter's House, London Grip, Mslexia, The North, Orbis, Poetry News, Spelt, Stand, Strix, Live Canon Anthology* (2017), *Bread & Roses Anthologies (*2019 & 2020), *RAY Refugee Anthology* (2020), *Doncaster Read 2 Write Anthology* (2020), *Wagtail: The Roma Women's Poetry Anthology* (2021). Several poems first appeared in my pamphlets *Bloodlines* (Seren Books, 2020) and *The Last Dinosaur in Doncaster* (Smith|Doorstop, 2021).

'Trip to the National Portrait Gallery, with the wife' won the *Mslexia* Poetry Competition 2016; 'Things My Mother Taught Me' won the Red Shed 2016; 'Blood Sugar' won the Poetry Society Stanza Competition 2021; 'Bloodlines' came second in the Ledbury Poetry Festival Competition 2019; 'Giant Leaping' came second in the Wirral Festival 2013; '*Pitched early mornin' at encampment o' Gypsy king Esau Smith*' placed third in the Black Country Museum Prize 2016; 'Shelling Peas with My Grandmother in the Gorgiolands' longlisted in the National Poetry Competition 2018 and came third in The Plough 2021; 'The Ring' was a runner-up in *Mslexia*/PBS 2019; 'Carroty Kate' shortlisted in the Keats-Shelley 2018; and 'The Bittern' was highly commended in *The Rialto* Nature and Place Competition 2018. 'The Lost' shortlisted in the Live Canon 2017 Poetry Competition and was performed by Nichole Bird, Live Canon Ensemble:
https://www.youtube.com/watch?v=0RCw-dUkRek

'In the Library' is a response to Channel 4's 2012 advertising campaign for *Big Fat Gypsy Weddings* – '*Bigger. Fatter. Gypsier.*' It was ruled as offensive and banned by the Advertising Standards Authority.

'William Shaw is lowered down the shaft' is based on the inquest which recorded that while working at Tinsley Park Colliery Sheffield, my great-great grandfather, William Shaw, fell out of the hoppit and drowned at the shaft bottom.

'STOP!' is a response to the photograph: J1312ms15.jpg, taken by John Harris during the Miners' Strike in 1984 when miners barricaded Rossington Colliery. www.reportdigital.co.uk

Thank you to the inspiring and supportive poets and organisations I have met along the way: York Stanza, especially Carole Bromley, Stuart Pickford and Phil Connolly; York Explore; Mick Jenkinson, Ian

Parks and Doncaster Read 2 Write; David Morley, Jane Draycott and all at Arvon 2019; Charlotte Wetton, Freya Jackson, Penny Newell, Clare Pollard, and The Garsdale Retreat; Wirral Poetry Festival and Joe Williams; Ledbury Poetry Festival; Jo Clement and the ERIAC Roma Women's Poetry Workshops 2020; the Society of Authors for their support and New Writing North for my Northern Writers' Award.

Special thanks to Lucy Doyle, for the kind use of her incredible artwork, *Shelling Peas*. http://www.lucydoyle.com

I am particularly grateful to Amy Wack and Seren; *Mslexia* and the Poetry Book Society; Ann and Peter Sansom and The Poetry Business, and Neil Astley at Bloodaxe for making this book possible.

POETRY FILMS

The following films were produced by my lovely Dad (filmmaker) and Mum (props, bit-parts and occasionally allowed to point the camera) which kept us in touch during Covid lockdowns:

'Near Extinction': https://www.youtube.com/watch?v=wFSQQxqb3sk

'The Pencil Sharpener', shortlisted in the 2021 Ó Bhéal Poetry-Film competition: https://www.youtube.com/watch?v=jSwrTdCJK3k

'I can see Sandbeck Hall':
https://www.youtube.com/watch?v=5PVjMVv2OAc

'Late Afternoon by a Hedge', included in Ilkley Literature Festival's Digital Fringe Showcase 2020: https://www.youtube.com/watch?v=Z0OHixkvX8U&t=21s

'Pilgrim Queens' was written in response to Rachel Carter's *Spirit of the Mayflower* Pilgrim Women sculptures with Doncaster Read 2 Write and produced as a sound-scape by Posey in Motion. This was then made into a poetry film, including print work by chronic doodler and community printmaker, Stephen Lee Hodgkins:

https://www.youtube.com/watch?v=iIJ6y-D6JLs

https://www.rachelcarter.co.uk/projects

https://www.instagram.com/poesy_inmotion

http://stephenleehodgkins.net

'Bloodlines' was produced as a poetry-film by Isobel Turner:
https://isobel-rose.wixsite.com/home